Praise for

BURNT SPOON
BURNT HONEY

In his startling debut, Anthony Aguero's language is an 'urgent hush,' a 'hunger breaking flesh.' He dismantles sentimentality, complicates the familial, and unravels queer desire. His poems make visible the full spectrum of human existence. Addiction, love, pain, and lust are intertwined into beautifully crafted lines that sing, that mourn. Aguero's lyrical intelligence is instructive and courageous. I'm grateful for this book.

— **Eduardo C. Corral**, author of *Guillotine*

Poignant, lyrical, and driven by language both honest and engaging, Anthony Aguero's *Burnt Spoon Burnt Honey* takes a close look at the nuances of familial and intimate relationships—how they're formed; how they become strained; how they leave us feeling as empty as they do full. Here, Aguero's speaker examines the consequences of his "spine always in search of memory," and how his "hunger [for] breaking flesh" turns into reflections that don't always yield clear answers. What does it mean when God has gone from your father's hands? How do you make love to someone who inflicts hurt upon your body? How do you cope with feeling constantly like you don't belong? Even though the speaker might come to the conclusion that "love is a complex thing" that might never be understood, he knows that the journey of self-discovery cannot be carried out without offering every last ounce of body, mind, and soul. Prepare to accept poems that are meaningful and tender.

— **Esteban Rodriguez**, author of *The Valley*

Love and violence share space so often in Anthony Aguero's *Burnt Spoon Burnt Honey*, it's hard to tell them apart. Many sentiments could be assigned to such a blurring, but the poems in this collection restlessly render that reality at the same time they refuse the resignation often associated with normality. Aguero's speaker discloses, "I wanted my history untouched and unedited. There is a myth that if I cracked my heart onto the concrete in my hometown and showed you the pieces, you'd see no blood." This collection faithfully collages boyhood and manhood, family and friendship, sex and sexuality, and illness and addiction, arcs that are often co-opted to make mythology of Black and brown existence, but there's every reason to trust Aguero and his speaker when he says, "Today, I offer something tender." *Burnt Spoon Burnt Honey* is an entirely heartfelt delivery of that promise.

— **Dustin Pearson**, author of *A Season in Hell with Rimbaud*

In Anthony Aguero's debut collection, *Burnt Spoon Burnt Honey*, you'll find salvation and shimmering--and every shade of dark that overlaps between these worlds. These poems are the ghosts of loss, and the reforming of a self through image and body and tongue. They are that of a missing father, a transgressed mother, and the confused hands that shuffle it all back into memory. Each stanza is a fragmented offering, "a litany/ of burns throughout his body," and the holy smoke that plumes afterwards. These are the ruptures and "cracked teeth," the untender paralyzations that stick with us after we've witnessed certain traumas. But do not be misled: within hurt, hides "the grandiosity of oceans"; within chaos, we find a "pretty moon." As Aguero assures himself, and us: "My body sung its undeath." Listen to his singing-that sacred act of unburying the deepest truths.

— **Alan Chazaro**, author of *Piñata Theory*

Burnt Spoon
Burnt Honey

FLOWERSONG
PRESS

poetry by

ANTHONY AGUERO

FLOWERSONG
PRESS

FlowerSong Press
Copyright © 2022 by Anthony Aguero
ISBN: 978-1-953447-40-1
Library of Congress Control Number: 2022932260

Published by FlowerSong Press
in the United States of America.
www.flowersongpress.com

Cover Image Credit/ Cover Design Credit:
Alexander AD | www.alexander.co

Author Photo Credit: Amiah

Set in Adobe Garamond Pro

NOTICE: SCHOOLS AND BUSINESSES
FlowerSong Press offers copies of this book at quantity discount with bulk
purchase for educational, business, or sales promotional use. For information,
please email the Publisher at info@flowersongpress.com.

CONTENTS

4   Nothing Holy About the Land

5   [My dad is in the garage…]

6   History

7   Hierarchy of Hunger

8   1992

10 The First Man I Loved

11 Tio

12 Tía

14 The Light Casts a Shadow Like

16 500 Square Foot

17 I'm Tired of Thinking of My Father

20 Human Immunodeficiency Virus

21 Undetectable Explained to a Primo

22 Amends

23 Papier-mâché

24 I Don't Want to Die

25 Several Birds Crossing My Mind at Once

26 My Therapist Asks Why I Didn't Deserve the Assault

27 My Body

28 Seroconversion Under the Covers

30 Today I Offer Something Tender

32 I Take His Body

33 Many Definitions of Clean

35 I Would've Done Anything

37 He Begins With My Body

38 His Profile Says He is Hunting

39 Being Whole After a Diagnosis

42 Christian

44 Burnt Spoon/ Burnt Honey

45 Dominique

47 Exile Returning to Me for Years

48 History of Meth

49 Something Holy is in That Bag

50 Amphetamine

52 Everyone Wants to Tell Me How to Be Alone

53 Now That You've Met God, Where to Go From Here

55 Behind Closed Doors

57 Ezequiel

58 The Shape of My Dreams

60 These Scars, Mine

61 So I Am a City

62 The Sound the Body Makes Hitting the Concrete

63 Litany of Making Love When It'll Kill You

64 O These Titles We Inherit

66 Self-Appraisal

68 Crack Towers in Palm Springs

69 Eyes Covered While Licking the Grease From My Fingertips

71 Before the Drugs

72 I Defended You

73 The Leaves in the Tree Are Looking a Lot Like Shadows

75   Someone Says They'd Take a Bullet for You

76   Every House in Palm Springs Imagined As A Place I've [ ]

77   He Wants to Have a Conversation On Rolling Veins

78   Imagine Being That Elegant

79   I Was

for Mom

Burnt Spoon
Burnt Honey

I

I was never safe, even when I was most hidden.
Even then I was waiting.

— Louise Glück

Nothing Holy About That Land

No, God's
    been gone
    from Dad's
    hands. A

Wrench's been
    lunged in
    the center
    of myself,

And I've spilt
    all the light
    that's left
    of his *O*.

We talk of him;
    heartache
    of my *O* and
    kitten tongue,

Like he is here.
    You hear
    his cleaver
    in my hand?

No, God's
    been tending
    his growling
    deep-throat.

And I've spilt
    the memory
    of all his
    slaughters.

[My Dad is in the garage preparing the glass]

My Dad is in the garage preparing the glass,

And by preparing the glass; I don't mean he's dead.

I just mean blowtorch and flammable things like hair

Or skin or paper-thin words slitting the lonely tongue.

Okay! Reprise. My Father is in the garage

Hunched over a piece of glass, broken glass, and he's

Sad like all of us are sad but doesn't make sound.

I'm in the garage with Dad, not making a sound,

Just being the attentive little good-boy, good-sport;

Just so so so good and the glass snaps and anger.

Now, he's angry and I'm sad and I don't make sound,

I just twiddle my thumbs and hope for the best and

I reprimand the drugs instead of him because

It's the glass — the hands as the prime agent of death.

History

It's dry here in my hometown.
The land has a history I'm unashamed to tell.
First, history with its nooks and holes.
I continually find myself asking him to imitate warmth.
The blanket. The hole-in-wall you think
to be degrading and primal, but there is that
leap of faith you are constantly asking of me.
I take it. I take it all. My skin cracking
under the pressure of history or this dry air.
The man on top of me is someone
I have tried to believe over and over.
That I should not have accepted the money
That I should be okay with what I had
and have, but I want so much more. I want
his touch to be just that and nothing romantic.
I wanted to be able to tell you my story.
I wanted history and its unknowing holes
and its nooks and the man at the end
of a tunnel with his menacing gaze. I wanted
my history untouched and unedited.
There is a myth that if I cracked my heart onto
the concrete in my hometown and showed
you the pieces, you'd see no blood.

Hierarchy of Hunger

My dad burned most of our memorabilia
From childhood — just like that, poof,

A snake crawls between my thighs

And excretes the poison, I mean love,
I mean *Here are my images*

Bathed in sunlight — gone.
A man sucks the vitamin E from my body

And massages the place a scar should be.
Here are my lips: red and aroused.

I try to remember a litany of hungers:

The first and last drug as actual serpent.
A series of fires on a cold, cold night.
How I bite into the neck of man's body.

My spine always in search of memory.
The sound of my hunger breaking flesh.

1992

I was about seven when I first watched
my grandmother climb into my mom's bed.
I saw her put her hands around mom's throat

like a gardener to a weed in a rose bush.
I didn't fully understand what was happening.
Love is a complex thing I never understood.
My father with sharp grass in his teeth
and half-truths that came and came

just like the man I thought I loved.
An intense feeling of deep affection
says the paper so prone to tears and the
inability to produce a wince or rebuttal

or packed bags or a yelling match or
clothes on fire or passionate love or
the roses clipped or the clock ticking or
someone to talk to or sinking to the bottom

of the pool and taking in all that air after or
the option of falling in love all over again or
writing or poetry or communication or
how to walk away when the moon is out.

I never know when the moon is out anymore.
I am always trying to catch love in the act.
In an angry act. In a passionate act.

In an unholy act. In a monstrous act.
Theatrical, infant, unconditional, or
conditional act. In any act really, just so
I can watch the moon again. Just to
get my mother's scream out of my head

and more celestial objects and
more to the books. But that's not love.
Love is out in the garden, waiting,
to be plucked alive.

The First Man I Loved

Wasn't my father. He was busy tending
to other things: the God bouncing around in his
delusion, an oil-burner turned into paraphernalia,
and/ or mistress(es) for his misogynistic daydreams,
his hand dancing over a flame for affect and
bunny-shadows to see if he could make me laugh,
breathing in an array of scents: drain-o, pickled antlers,
matchsticks grounded for séance, and a séance
to bring back his former life. I laughed, yes,
at the shadows he casted on the industrialwall
of his garage with the adhesive that
solidified like the calcium building up on his
molars from opening too many sweets
for me. I laughed because, maybe, I'm delusional.
But more about him. You're aware by now
that my father's incredibly preoccupied
with a devil in a clown car that he believes
carries the entire lineage of his ancestry, but
I told him it's just the ice cream truck making
its second round around the neighborhood.
There's no bandanna that'll contain the pool
of sweat he's managed to create through
intense attentiveness to looking for that thing:
that one thing, that shapeless thing,
that either living-or-non-living entity thing,
that thing with that one color and
Anthony, have you seen that fucking thing?
but this is where I've learned persistence.
I was completely awe-struck the day he
bellowed out a dense cloud, one that seemed
a dam-about-to-break, and I was prepared
for a flood, and isn't God controller of the weather?
and isn't God meant to be the first man I loved?

Tío

Tells me beware
of the River Styx,
that there is
always a current
rushing nearby
and, suddenly,
a spill of water.
Oxalises sprout:
one on his mouth,
a crack of the
tooth, a rupture
of the lung, and
one in my hand.
Tells me of a
man in a coat,
waiting, spilt spit,
and foreboding.
Yellowed-skin.
Sour tongue,
cursing the past:
beware the River
Styx. Glass liver
thrown against,
caught under, a
current of the
hospital gurney.
Water, water
rushed nearby,
flower plucked
from a man's
dying words.

Tía
After Aracelis Girmay

There was a portrait of you.
You, wrapped in deep-blue

Ocean fur. I wondered over
Your laugh, like a belch but

Regal and soft: all the birds
Responding. Oh, your blood,

Ours, all of us, not allowing you
Or I, the promise of health;

Of abundance like rivers and
Lakes. The gaze of your eyes

Appears to be saying— Tell me
About the pain, transfusions,

Your body rejecting the nectar
Of a ripe guayaba. I wanted

To meet you at the border-point
Between California and Mexicali;

Between this life and the one
That follows so stealthily.

Tell me *When you listen to a*
Body of water, do you hear songs

Too? Oh, but you are here. Listen,
Hear, the mourning dove perched

Alongside the home you've lived.
Here, the home you've lived now

A multitude of this life and the
One that comes after and after,

A stretch of blue more continuous
Than the grandiosity of oceans.

Borders drowned under the gaze
Of a portrait of you, uninterrupted,

And, now,
gone.

The Light Casts a Shadow Like
My Dad Does When On Drugs

A short eclipse
of his body

    in almost
    reverence.

Look, look at me!
how my pupils eclipse.

Folklore
chemical
mythology -

    He sung of a trinity
    while his spine bent

the patterns of
any monster
of any body
misinterpreted.

    There's a garden under
    the blanket of his eyelids.

The solemn
slant of his eye
shot upward.

    A tragedy it was, all
    that light turned-away.

His body
in almost
astronomical
proportions.

There's a story arc I'd
prefer not to get into.

The change in the
sea of his voice.

An autumn lasted in his
petty throat where seasons
failed to exist.

500 Square Foot

I love you, electric
stove, 30 squarefoot
kitchenette,
I love you. Alone,
gone, cooked in
the Hamburger
Helper, I love you,
steady hands
snapping twigs,
or cilantro stems,
or scraping the
surface of my skin.
I love you, pretty
moon, pretty mom,
difficult brothers,
I love you too. Find
these words on
their way to you.
Four by four box, I
snap you in place,
I love you too,
inventive creation
of the 500 square
foot. I extend my
embrace and take
you all inside me.
I love you, I am
sorry, so sorry, I
was angry; myself,
with nowhere to
howl, pretty moon.

I'm Tired of Thinking of My Father

Someone asked if I was okay the other day.
Objectively, yes. I comfortably could have
Said there were about two and a half meals
Scattered throughout the day because I was
Likely hungry. It reminded me of a checkbox
Inquiring about my appetite followed by the
Question of wanting to harm myself or not.
Suffice it to say, I can't even put myself back into
The last time I used drugs. But I could provide
A vivid detail of the events that occurred.

Growing up, we had various animals, all at
Different stages of the years. All of them
At the mercy of the neighbor's vicious dogs.
Princess, Aflack, all those chickens in the
Chicken coop, and a rabbit whose name
Eludes me to this day.

My therapist checks in every time I see him
By asking *How are you feeling this morning?*
I waltzed into his office more times than not
With the walls spinning because of the prior
Evening dancing into dehydration.
The answer was almost always that I was fine.

Honesty has its way of slipping through my
Fingers, and I'd like to blame my father.
But I won't. I don't remember how it was the
First time eating cake, but I'd imagine
It was the same as swindling myself out of a
Situation through biting my tongue.

I'm not a dishonest person.
Life just teaches you to the keep the knife
Behind your back

And peel the apple directly in front of
The stranger and to smile. Always a smile.

I prefer listening to r&b or neo-soul because
It relaxes the soul.

If someone asks if I'm okay the first thought is
I'm tired of thinking of my father. Sisyphus,
I would like to believe, had the shape of him.
A trick up the sleeve. A disappearing trick.
A trick for the ages. A trick even I'd believe.
You see, I am exhausted of the hill he and I
Built together. And the stone in my chest,
It doesn't get any lighter.

The animals in the yard have all become ghosts.

I keep checking off boxes lately that suggest
I'm doing just fine.
Sorry for milling around the yard so long.
I think I'm ready to come home.

II

I'm, you know, still here,
tulip, resin, temporary—

— Jean Valentine

Human Immunodeficiency Virus

I think about you so often I wonder if I am
        in love with you but

I won't say I'm in love with you

No   Never

The first person to teach me about it

       gifted me
a flesh-light, all pink and cotton candy

Said *Wherever you take this*

            Think of me

I thought of him
        as a tree stripped of its

branches   and naked
                of leaves

He leaves me
       a gift   a virus

all night sweats and tremor and endless

O the urgency
        of having to love you

just to keep myself   alive

Undetectable Explained to a Primo

What does it mean, you know, to you?

I massage a rose petal onto each temple
And breathe in its perfume.

So, you're like taking care of yourself, right?

My body discovering song.

But I mean can you, like, give it to
Anyone else?

A bird ate from my hand and fluttered away.

Can you be in love with anyone else?

In this lifetime and next and next and—

I guess what I'm trying to ask is
Does it bother you that I'm asking?

My hands using a rosary as expression;
As the blood I'm trying to help you see.

So, you like, take medication every day?

A rose petal floating down my esophagus.

I mean, like, what does it mean to you?

My body sung its undeath.

Amends

A man I used to sleep with
believed himself to be a ghost.
Put his hands underneath my damp
shirt and kissed me amongst
the mosquitoes swarming his pickup.
This meant I was clearly a god.
Skin built omnipotent and brown
and, then, under-aged. I wanted
understanding the way I knew
my body swelled when touched
or, at least, exposed to the buzz
just outside his heap of metal.
So he was a ghost who's had his way.
Vanishes – a swell on my inner left calf
tells me I wasn't a god all along.

Papier-mâché

My skin is not the regular skin.
Just last week, I spit up paper
that I swallowed
a while back. My mom said it
isn't normal. There's something
in the way I can't always breathe
on my own.
My skin not on its own.
My skin under another man.
My skin torn like paper
when handled with improper
hands. Hands improper
only when burnt on each side.
Hands improper
if and when I can't find the
thing you're asking for.
Stop asking.
Back to skin. My skin.
Not the regular type of skin.
The petals kept in place.
The breath kept constant.
The scars, healed.
How I closed my eyes to
rip another sheet of paper.
How you can call that ugly.
My skin.

I Don't Want to Die

I don't want to   die.   Maybe,
other options: burnt orchid,
                                   burnt burnt orange peel,
                                   tooth unreeling,
                                   burning heart. &

Maybe, I'm chucking a bullet to the moon. Burnt,

burnt crater   adhering
to the wishes of my mouth: burnt wishbone.

Maybe, undying   as *A* or *B*
                                  as zest splintered
                                  as burnt burnt burnt

I don't want to die. Maybe,
I don't. Maybe, I
live & maybe I watch
                          a beautiful endless
                          burn,
                          burn — Pretty burning.

No, I live.

Several Birds Crossing My Mind At Once

It's hard to imagine
  anything dying,

    especially the mind: memory
      only a breathing mirror

with a thousand scratches
  of clawed marks.

    Like the body begging to
      return

to the fine incision of
  a papercut,

    but the blood coagulates
      all over the glass —

all those birds pecking
  at their last meal.

    This premeditated flinching
      as everything, at once,

crosses my mind.
  My only grievance was not

    allowing those birds
      inside this chest.

My Therapist Asks Why I Didn't Deserve the Assault

Night breezes seem to whisper I love you. I am
trying to discern the rind of a peach

from a coyote's fur dragging a
in the desert I no longer belong to. *Dream*

a little dream of me I still no longer belong to.
My eyes close, and the grass stabbing me near

death. These ghosts all coming back
in restitution. *While I'm alone and blue as can be.*

I wanted to believe the blood was warmer on
the outside of the body than inside, all of this

taken up complacent-matter. *Stars fading, but*
I linger on dear, and the ghosts are asking for

blood at the door, by name, so we should let them
in because even tears themselves become tired.

Sweet dreams that leave all worries behind you
when the breath trickles down to the sound of

footsteps against the gravel in a desert when
a man leaves with wisps of hair. Oh, the safety

of a night breeze. *Stars fading, but I linger on*
dear, and unaware of any other variation

of my body saying no. *Night breezes seem to*
whisper I love you, blood-stain kisses on a shirt.

My Body

My body under a body
under another body
under multiple bodies
under a tower under
a lock of flowering curled hair.

My body under
a body under another body
under your body
under the waft of horse
and vanity. My body
under a body under another body under
a carcass left to decay for a thousand years
with a lost autopsy report indicating
asphyxiation and a waiver

signed, crumpled inside his
feeble chest. My body
under his body under another body under my
body, again, but this time the body
       as cavern;   as horse;   as stench;
      as hoe; and
           it just might be my body.

Seroconversion Under the Covers

The kettle on the stove had
        been whistling for days

and nobody attempted to
        turn it off

I was under a thicket of
        warm covers when I
only wanted a thin-sheet

My ears had been bleeding
        with the run-off of sweat

I'd collected in a coffee jar.
        Surely, I was dying.

The heat of the room
        ploughing into my chest

I wanted a thin sheet and
        the screeching to stop.
I was imagining things:

Winter snow draped over
        my exposed toes;

The smell of cinnamon from
        the room next door meant
I wasn't dying.

But I was dying
        and nobody turned it
off.

And I hadn't a name for you,
        inaudible disposition

A pile of bodies wrapped
      atop of me
Nobody was safe
      Not even me

Today I Offer Something Tender

Because I have forgotten of my body

As something *there*

I offer light in the form of a beam

Of lighthouse

As a form of escape

Because there is such thing as escape

I dig a door

Just above the naval

And I ask you to enter gently

Without waking the four-tailed beast.

Or I ask you to enter violently

Distracting the thing asleep so

I may leave

When I think of assault

I think lighthouse in flames

Four-tailed beast

A door entering into me

Sex with any man

The smell of a matchbook on fire

An endless sentence

Today I offer something tender

Because I have misplaced my body.

I Take His Body

I take his body.
What is
The earliest
Memory
Of the assault?
His legs. The dick.
The apple fallen
from his thighs
The building and
it's brown,
my brown
His breath
His sound
Shuffling upward
in a hurry
to silence the
crunch
of my bite.
My bite. My brown.
My sound hurrying
for an exit
for a plea
I take his body
everywhere
with me
my voice goes.

Many Definitions of Clean

First, undirty.

    Body, scrubbed raw

Until bled dry.

    Cured meat on a

blessed slab.

    How to harvest that

which is already dead.

    Dried petals to

completely cover
    the body.

    Something cold

turned warm.

    Coffee drunk

black — sweet milk.

    Wide, open throat

without lesions

    or cracked branches.

Blood preserved

lipstick-red in vials.

Untouched spine of
   his book(s).

In conclusion,

   undirty.

I Would've Done Anything

I would've done anything because it's love, right?
I would've clipped my peaches in quarters and
fed them to the parrots hoping they'd mimic
their sweetness.
I would've sucked his dick because he asked
and because that is romance.
I would've stomped the ground, shoes and all,
just to recognize how my body rises against his
when anger is all that we have left.
I would've taken off his shirt and made it sensual.
I would've bottomed and I'd declare it unforgettable but
I would've known the truth and let my shoulders
slouch. I'd call that love too.
I would've traced my index finger
along the crease of his crotch and he'd have gone crazy.
I would've put that same finger across my naval, then chest,
and say *This, this, is where I remain empty.*
I would've said *Action* and now we're in a movie,
and I'm Drew Barrymore because isn't that irresistible.
I would've bitten into the already bitten peach
hoping I could come across bitable.
More in place. More just right. More body ready and willing.
I would've read him telling poetry.
I would've softened my edges.
I would've handed the knife over and said *Aqui mismo,*
but the power would have gone out and
I would've been reminded, again, of powerlessness.
I would've never allowed him to advance a few spaces.
I would've done anything but I didn't.
I would've flapped my shoulder-blades and fluttered off.
I would've reminded myself over and over
that which I did not deserve.
I would've used absolutes sparsely, almost never.

I would've said *My body, my body, my body.*
I would've allowed my body to reject his hand
over my mouth. I would've done anything.

He Begins With My Body

Says *I'm not picky.*
Says *I'll eat just about anything*
Except olives and how they remind him of a vulgar
entrance. How you tell me *I am trying to protect*
My body. How I allow you to take the power from
My fingertips. I am up in the middle of the night
Swallowing a jar of olives and
Burning the tips of each finger that told you
You deserve the world, sweetheart. You bitter kiss.
I imagine pouring vinegar all over the diagnosis.
I imagine my spit on the ground instead
Of your mouth. I wanted to shout.
Olives are required to endure a curing process
Before they can enter the body.
To be taken in raw.
To taste the bitter core.
To have given you exactly what you wanted.
Plopped into the mouth with no after-
Thought. Without desire, but hunger
All of that hunger.
There are two methods to the curing process.
I have one. Only one. Always one.
Says he's not picky. Says his body isn't ready.
I am just trying to protect my body,
But I am not ready to rest in a layer of salt
You have laid out for me.

His Profile Says He is Hunting

And I am immediately swept back to the time my
Tio Joe shot a pig in the head and all that blood had
Nowhere to run but into an unused bathtub tucked
Neatly in the far back of the land my Grandfather
Has owned since just after the war, a war, his war.
Since every war is something personal when you're
Placed in the middle of it all happening, blazing in
Your ear.

And I am immediately swept back to the time my
Same Tio guts the pig in front of our innocent eyes,
The same way that same man has intended for my
Body. The same body that has wrung itself in hopes
For a second chance. My war. My ears hot and
Blazing and waiting for what is wrong with my body.
He handles the pig's skin indirectly and impersonal.
Your skin.

And I am immediately swept back to the time my
Tio Joe didn't cry when he took this pig's life,
I wonder if every war begins with a man in hunt.
I wonder if he looks at my body and wonders the
Safest place to point the gun. I wonder how he
Defines the term clean. The meat, tender, falling
Softly off the bone. His personal vendetta, his war.
Your turn.

Being Whole After A Diagnosis

I. Diagnosis

Someone likens your body to soured-meat,
Flies swarming the thighs, a hint of cinnamon
Brushes just underneath your nose.

ELISA has confirmed the inevitable.
O you enzyme-linked immunosorbent assay.

II. Treatment Plan

Someone says take this ad infinitum. One by one,
Opal, green pills sitting at the bottom of a valley.
Nothing violet or green ever growing.

Stribild was approved by the US FDA in August 2012
For human bodies.
A cocktail of Vitekta, Tybost, Viread, and Emtriva.

III. Non-Adherence

Someone mentioned they smelled a thing dying
In the apartment you lived in. You checked each
And every corner - he put a flashlight
in your throat. Says *It's you*. You prepare
an *ofrenda* with only cinnamon sticks.

Immunocompromised. Death in the white-
Blood of my body.

IV. Reminder

Death likes to tap at the sole of your foot.
It smells of cinnamon just to confuse you.

You smell meat running its course.

V. Adherence

One by one, opal, green pills sprawling at the
Bottom of a translucent lake. Little by little,
The color rushing back into your body.

Antiretroviral treatment –
The ceasefire of replication.

VI. Being Whole After a Diagnosis

You drowned so many times just to get here.
A hint of cinnamon brushes just under your nose.
O the scent of living, too.

III

When did you first enter the territory of thirst?

— Natalie Diaz

Christian

I promised I wouldn't talk about ghosts again.
Something is rustling under my chest.

A church is alone in the middle of the desert.
Inside the desert, it smelled like your throat.

There's something to occupying space—
Something abandoned, living or righteous.
It doesn't matter since we're at grief.

My sight is rearranged to see spots of red.
To see your fingers as a match as you strike
The room ablaze with a single votive candle.

It requires an expedition to uncover and
Excavate the sight of any ruin. Help me.

Your apartment is still there.
Is still there, is still the same. Should we
Build an effigy of our living together?

I can't help you anymore
Lodged in my throat like melted rock.

Here I am, trying to rewrite a piece of
Paired ruin: the crash, reduction, a body
Revoked of its thirst.

I offer you the pool of my body to reverse
The infection crowding your narrowed throat.

The color of your pupils
Before the water drowns them again,
Forever.

The church is burning, it is in flames.
The dead have found the location of our ruin.

The kid of my tongue tastes a body too familiar.
I have to blow this candle out now.

I'm sorry. I promised.

Burnt Spoon/ Burnt Honey

Sugar-water
with powdered
dye. Hummingbirds
contain no sense of smell.
The sofa was on fire and
not once
did he inhale the scent,
just noticed
from the rear
all that brilliant red.
He could've died
burning up that spoon.
Honey dipped inside
a tub of lighter fluid.
A bouquet of red, orange,
and carmine streaked
across the shimmer
of his dead, cold eyes.
Sugar-water with
turned-over skin
he guzzles down
for nourishment;
to continue humming
to the sound of
that dying bird
flapping about inside
his charred chest.

Dominique

After Kaveh Akbar's,
"Orchids are Sprouting From the Floorboards"

I wanted so much for us

There's nothing more to describe

The metaphors that slip off of my tongue

I'm tired of the daggers you place at my back

There are flowers in your throat

that I'd have plucked for your mother

Even the flowers are glass, too, and

I wanted so, so much for us as well

Dominique, the fires smell really close

and I'm tired of the metal you pierced

in the hole of my chest. It burns, still

The drugs are no longer doing the trick:

that magic, that *Look, look! Heaven's falling*

I'm exhausted of the lurid colors we try

and emulate by licking our scars back raw

You carry lighters in your back-pocket

because it's both reckless and elegant

Love has taken on an ulterior motive for us

We're starting fires in the pit of our palms

that make the shape of wishes found in a well

All this stuff is flowing from our mouths

and this isn't expensive or warmth

You're beginning to fall asleep on the couch

The lotuses in Echo Park are on fire tonight
and I wish you were here to see them with me
Our bodies have become a sort of revelation
for the clocks in us that will, too, stop ticking
Quick the *Crystal* is going to *Go-Fast* and
these, our bodies, have swallowed too many
blades for any light-things to grow. *X*, death
There's a lot I'd care to say but you're looking
at the sun as if time is running out It is
Where do we go from here?

Exile Returning to Me for Years

We return to the
Site of tragedy. I am
Making love
To my very own
Perpetrator with
Hands like mine.
No more rage or
Carmine to strike
Me with: I apportion
His hands and
Appropriate its
Body defenseless.
No more blood I
Say. No more
Lurid strokes
'Til my arms fall
And I am, like once,
Back in a land
Of cringe and

       exile.

History of Meth

It begins with me, tanned-skin under
Many moons/ men. Ephedra plant
Tickling the underside of my belly
Until I release a belch and she seeps
Right in/ from under my contoured
Nose/ small, white lights like fireflies
Trapped on my tip. I sneeze. I laugh.
I wake. Skeleton in the shape of a
Fetus beckons me to leave this part
Of history/ of powdered angels/
Minced bones of so many deaths.
Man-made Azrael, Ephreda—
Substitue, Reaper of Sleep: how
You have conquered my histories.
Kissing the river of my veins, I come
For you/ I bleed/ I rip out my sacrum
And gift it to a man that, too, begins
With you. Your many names I try
Not speak. How you delude me into
Believing/ it begins with me.

Something Holy is in That Bag

F— finding God when I have this diamond:
my small sparkling incisor, cherubim crystals,
thing shoved in a condom inserted in rear
and we just met, but my blood is boiling.
O my white firefly buzzing in my ear.
I have trapped you in a mason jar and
moved us around in direction of the night —
how I have bound us, misery flushing out
all of our adopted light. The sound we both
make being shaken when encased
in stone, in dirt, in glass, in the story
I have never been capable of justifying:
I yanked out my back molar to replace it with
A substitute god. My diamond, my small
sparkling specter, you little cherubim crystals
with your wings clipped, flapping around and
looking for the smallest source of holy light.
O God, O God my blood has overflown and
all of the emaciated bodies are on fire.
My glass enclosure has cracked open and
this is what they meant by *a healthy fear.*
Here, my light is burning just outside a door.
Here, a thing higher than God, taker of lives,
the cry it makes crushed by a boot, my little
cherubim crystals, you yank out my tongue
and speak in your own unholy voice asking
for the rest of my body back. But it's mine.

Amphetamine

Peanut butter
and/ or jelly
sandwich

Tastes one
loves — salt
on the back
of a wrist/
his wrists

The plural
tragedies he/
they/ she
groaned over

Things one
loves — salt
at the
bottom of a
cornea

He scoops salt from a
dried, haunted lake to
dust in front of his gaze
unaware he is drying
his body to the same
fate of all that dust.

Songs of stark
and sweetness:
he had the most
beautiful skin.

The light from the fridge
had attracted a wolf, blood

running down the incisors:
it snarled with its devil eyes.

Jiffy Peanut Butter
Strawberry Jam:
melancholy of
tastes and loves.

One definitive
act of travesty
after another
after another
after –

Everyone Wants to Tell Me How to Be Alone

Wrong place. Wrong time. How to settle
for the wrong dream. Wrong wrist.
Wrong preference. Wrong skin.
Diving into the seawater that is really
a river. Wrong space. Wrong degree.
Wrong way of rolling r's. Wrong size.
Something created to read from right
to left. Wrong way to love. Wrong,
wrong disease. Wrong drugs. Wrong
choice of words. The way he was
gentle with me is what you need to do.
Try again. Wrong breath.
Wrong embrace. Wrong smell. Wrong
choices. How to wake up correctly.
How to cough up river water onto the
Wrong place.

Now That You've Met God, Where to Go From Here

Do not go to the room
       with the blinds sewn shut   [your hands]
The excuses will become inexplicable and
               grating, and [your hands]
     You will draw a
litany of veins across your body
Like a map [your hands] for anyone who
         seeks a river or fresh blood,
[my hands].

Do not speak to the ghost   [your ghost]
     resting outside your zealous head.
He is not real,
he is not real,   he is only [your ghost]
A Ziplock of cerulean-dust
       someone let loose.
And he is only as real
     as someone's weak faith
Has become [my ghost].

Do not follow   the Man with X's for eyes,
    he only relies
On the forgotten   maps of the world –
O'   My eyes.

Do not stare   endlessly
    at your reflection   [mine]
your pupils   will only remind you
    of the time they   [mine]
Kissed your irises   and   poisoned their depth
Sending   [mine]   you   into the deepest rest

Do not smell the white-orchid,
      for it is a pheromone
That knows no

limits to the damage   it'll cause

                    your sex to do.

Do not look for God with my hands
            somewhere in the cleanest of carpets,
For you   will find him,   my ghost,
and your   running
               will never end.

Behind Closed Doors

After reading the article in NY Times
"What Happened Inside Ed Buck's Apt."

A roach crawled about the ledge
of an expensive windowsill. *Keep*
the door open he says. The door
is shut and the windowsill is not
as expensive when the lights are
down. What is a predator to the
roach? What kills the body when
it hasn't asked for slaughter? I
only dream of killing the roach,
you see. Nuance of the windowsill
that is familiar with dead
things; that is less expensive in
the shadow of the lights dimmed;
that is scattered with insects I
should've noticed before while
the lights were beaming. He, too,
is a ghost. Dead man with hungry
veins. Dead man which says I can't
be killed. The lights shut off and
he's wearing a grin. Predatory.
There's a knife in his hand, whack,
cleave, spit; whack, leave, spit.
You're scaring me he says as the
roach scurries across his shoulders
which is also a windowsill that can't
break. Does anybody peer inside?
Can't you see I'm dying? A bug
crawls from inside of his mouth,
which is also a windowsill. Don't

you hear the screaming escape?
He peels the exoskeleton from the
roach and says *Now I'm invincible.*
But the windowsill says differently.

Ezequiel

Ezequiel and I would roar down the desert
streets singing the most hopeful
Taylor Swift lyrics because isn't hope whitenoise?
I believed us. I still believe it.
Every morning the coffee with its magic,
and I still believe it holds special properties:
how the creamer changes the color.
How I think of you at the drop of a pinthe
two of us in your truck with KCRW,
or how we bled out hoping someone would
see us. There's magic in the people I've met.
You plucked a key from my throat once
and found a room to dance around inside of.
I was eighteen with a knife in my hand and
a blindfold on: I lick the salt off my wrist.
You promised we'd escape.
I look for you in the crowded room,
the sound of keys rattling inside of me.
The sound still crackling in a distance.

The Shape of My Dreams

The desert tells me
    There isn't enough music
        In the world to fill your empty places.

The man singing a song into me and can't

        Even get me to hum back to him.
    The color of my body in a sea of white:
A piece of desert I carry in myself everywhere I go.

Aspects of the desert: unapologetically
    Missing something, exacerbated by high and low
        Temperatures. Teach me about the rising sun,

        Kiss my sticky skin. There isn't enough
    Anything in the world that'll fill my
Empty spaces:

Place your ear against my mouth
    And listen how there was once a river.
        A lot of the Yuha Desert has been cultivated

        Into agricultural land:
    I spit onto a man's tongue
And he spits up a honeydew seed.

I spit onto the tip of my hands
    And hope I recognize what I see.
        And I hope my thirst hasn't drunk the man

        Who sleeps alongside me. Torrential —
    Whispers the desert; my home; my body
As I recognize myself as once a river

Waiting to spill
            My own song sung
    back into myself.

These Scars, Mine

The first paper-cut and its act of not staying,
Deceitful em dash with your promise of
Setting a part scars that which I cannot erase.

That which I cannot erase but your act, still,
of not staying — the way in which you keep
hearing the tide even after you've drowned.

The manner in which I've drowned with its
intention of not staying. How it begs the
prompt What do you want, still, to be gone?

The emaciation of my collarbone holds only
a single scar, promise of setting apart that,
and I impose to the questioner I won't say

That which has no intention of lingering. Emdash
like a scar which is mine, all of mine. My
Learning of floating atop the water around me.

So I Am a City

And my lakes have been replaced with
reservoirs that are purely decorative. The
trees are being gutted and fed to a man
who has been starving for the last century.
His toenails have been laced with crimsonink
and, unbeknownst to him, is toxic.
The homes have been ravaged so deep
within me I'm unsure whether anything is
salvageable. Profligate is the soil of my
overused body that was exhausted at
the destruction a pair of human hands
are capable of. So, I am a city disregarded
of its gems: drought, drink, thirst, thirst,
as in the effect of a significant loss of
blood. A man has brutalized any promise
of correcting this endless lack of slake
my body must endure. Sisyphus as the
city which has undone and repaired and
repeat and repeat. I hold my body up
to the brilliant light, all my buildings
shimmering all at once. All that hope
becoming and becoming itself once again.

The Sound the Body Makes Hitting the Concrete

I picked out a piece of flint from my nail
    And flicked it to the ground
   Asserting my right to make a wish:

     Mercy, if you must be a song —
Reach the rest of our dead.
   Wrap yourself along my tongue.

    And let me be prophecy.
Remember who first gave you voice.
I cannot hear you with a mouth-

Full of blood. Remind, all others,
    this is not a love song.
  I have witnessed heaven on the seventh day
    and it was a lurid pit of dark.

   All those pretty bodies hitting the pavement.
All those mouths attempting to call upon
   Mercy with a mouth-full of blood.

Litany of Making Love When It'll Kill You

My tongue as an instrument.
The smell of unclean hair.
How often you pick at your face.
The droop of your shoulders.
How defeat looks from a distance.
You making love to my voicemail.
Me making love to someone.
The crush of glass under a boot.
How a ribbon unravels mid-flight.
The coiling of a snake in hiding.
A mouth-shaped scar you leave.
My tongue as a ribbon landing.
The smell of my brown skin cleaned.
What makes a lover invalid?
How this virus multiplies.
This green, opal pill as an instrument.
Someone protecting their body.
A snake biting my neck.
How the poison spread.

O These Titles We Inherit

The first email I created began with *gettingspunky*
According to a then-friend, this would be suggestive
To those I was mass-messaging through ads on
Craiglist in the Palm Springs area.
This would imply I'd be a thorn in the disguise of
A sweet dove. Or that I could write a proper
Sentence on the experience and, therefore,
Definition of grit: my nail-beds filled with the salt
And earth of a man's spit. My nature is a hoe.
My thighs appropriate as a set of wings.
My body a *thing* you want to create word of.

The first time I swallowed a crystal in its entirety
I was sure that I could've offered you magic;
That my nights could've been spent with spells
And rebuilding the mysticism of my identity.
Instead,
I spread myself towards the east and west
Wondering if I'd find myself back at home. I'd
Put on a variety of disguises: profile name(s),
Different email addresses, force the flush of my
Skin because of my back turned from the sun,
And how I'd demand to a stranger *This is who
I am*. The first onyx-horned creature scraping
Against a bathroom window. I smashed my fist
Into myself.

A man once spoke of my body in terms of *gold*
And *worth*. I remember not asking for a lot.
Just enough to get me home are my demands.
He suggested I was only a snake, so I bit his neck
Hoping he would be writhing at my power. Instead,

He moaned and buried my body under his weight.
O, these titles we inherit
When I submit myself as prey; as stranger in the
Cold crying out to the moon as to where I belong.

Self-Appraisal

Do you find me handsome? Beauty, well,
that's in the eye of the beholder. I'd prefer
to start at the scent: the smell of earth in
the grip of strong hands, or the way you
preferred not to own any perfumes or
deodorants that might deter the pungent
pit of a male. *Do you find me handsome?*
You liked the boys is what
you had alluded to: their gush of wind
rushing past your face, but it was all a
heavily-curated pornography that you
probably shouldn't have owned at home.
So this meant you were ugly - you knew it.
Do you find me tolerable? Like abstraction,
it's hard to find these questions easy to
answer. However, once, I had sex with a
man. After, he texted me *Sex was great.*
Safe to say that answer is yes: tolerable.
Do you find me desirable? I wish I was one
to had picked up the craft of cigarette
smoking. Life would've been one grand,
gay noir film. Instead, I'm batting my eyes
hoping you get the first taste of honey out
of them. *Do you find me handsome?* What
I wanted was to unfold like the triptych of
a much-anticipated Playgirl edition, but
I'm over here shaking hands with a little
oomph as if saying *Check out this sexy,*
stern handshake. Nobody is paying attention
because nobody has time for that silly stuff.
I'm at the discretion of a vanity mirror
(metaphorically speaking) checking it all.
Do you find me handsome? Yes, gosh,
that beauty! (I am the beholder, naturally)
Do you find me tolerable? Baby, I wish I

could set this silly question into flames.
Do you find me desirable? Well, go ahead,
flex both forearms. See which one's stronger.
Then I turn the lights off after a thorough
self-appraisal of the body during doubt.

Crack Towers in Palm Springs

Among us were like-minds and lovers/
wearing cherry-pit lipstick/ with a demons
growl/ at the swallow of each our throats.
Fraternal twins that looked/ too alike/ their
bodies as a set of electronics/ deconstructed/
like god's garden on the first/ day of havoc
or creation/ depending on what Christian
is asked./ A Jetson's dystopia/ of flying discs
and fabricated creatures/ and a set of multifaceted/
screens for crimes/ of passion and/
the tongue/ that soft extension/ pulled out/
like a fruit roll-up/ and eaten whole./ An
entire troposphere at ground-level. Small
fires/ emblazoned on those/ empty gazes/
like a forsaken epitaph./ They wanted a
God/ and built Olympia with metal and
copper wire/ taken from their Mom's veins.
They kissed/ each other's backs/ with
fissured and bleeding lips/ attempting a
remembrance of/ the erect body that
once was./ Batteries spat out their mouths.

Eyes Covered While Licking the Grease From My Fingertips

I wanted to be so-strong so I thought
I would will myself a herniated disc
without the actual heavy-lifting.
Instead, I popped open a bottle of
cheap wine and expressed all my
feelings because I'm emotional or
I'm empathetic or I'm sensitive and
I've been touching myself all wrong
these past few months. No, no, no.
There wasn't any fucking involved,
fucking was practically nonexistent.
I was having a cappuccino, iced, no
froth at the top so I might've well asked
for a latte instead, but I wanted to try
and prove a point: I'm getting somewhere,
and I'm getting there sensibly.
But my clothes were off at some point.
I had, essentially, a latte in my hand. I
gave you the air of a body in importance.
Let me teach you about being pragmatic
the voice on speakers seem to say, but
I was naked and couldn't be bothered.
My skin was all greased up and I had

been flexing in the mirror because I want
to show you where I'm off to. Where I'm
going. Where you said I'd never land.

Before the Drugs

You are a big responsibility. I am trying
to all too often. That time, beneath the arms
of a large sequoia; my lips to yours, not kissing
but, simply, sharing breath — again. I'm kidding.

That time, you said *My heart is stopping*, your lips
dry, your skin dry, the sky, too, cracking high
high above our two small heads. Plath writes,
somewhere, *You smile./ No it is not fatal*
and I'm now shaking my empty head No, no!

You smile while we have taken things too far,
too far for what the living do with their hands.
Now, your voices are cracking. Now, the dark seeds
in my chest are pushing their way out. I told you,

I did, *Once we begin, there is no turning back.*

I Defended You
After Chuck R.

My friend
I smelled your
Shirt and it
Smelled of
Poppy-seed and
Let me kiss
Your teeth, again,
And turn the shower
Down.
Let's savor this
Scent once more.
My friend
I smelled your
Hands, and
I defended you,
And the fire
Was left running.
My friend,
You burned the field
And stayed.
You,
My friend,
You've gone.

The Leaves in the Tree Are Looking a Lot Like Shadows

Someone says
    Chemically-induced psychosis
under a hush;
      in a whisper; and suddenly,
          I am vexed
        because the leaves
in the tree
      are looking a lot like
          shadows.
Upon further inspection
          it was just a man
            with a blow-torch
        staining glass
perched on a branch.
          But a breeze
           swept through,
    briefly,
      and gave shape
to a wheezing-siren.
          I bawled and whimpered
   and   pleaded
           for it to stop.
        It was like this
     often of the time:
this becoming
    and unbecoming
          of small,
insignificant tragedies.
        Another interruption
        of the leaves
beckons me to peak
        Closer
    Closer
Look here
    the minotaur

with starry-eyes
                huffs the scent of my skin
and rejects
        my loss
                        of sanity.
                Then it's a face
        and a palace
                                an endless maze
and we're in hell.
                Then
                I'm
        drowning.

And I'm spitting
                myself from myself.
                        A gust of wind
                blows through,
        again,
                                and I am vexed.
        A whisper,
                an urgent hush
asking how to get off this tree.

Someone Says They'd Take a Bullet for You

You're too much.
That shirt is too loose.
That shirt is too tight.
Fix your smile, a little
higher.
Hold my back, it hurts.
Too much identity.
Too little.
You sound so alone.
Stop knowing.
Take me serious.
Crack my ribs,
Watch what grows.
You're too much.
You're too
Self in stone.
Crack open.

Every House In Palm Springs Imagined As A Place I've [   ]

Every house in Palm Springs was my first.
Every house in Palm Springs has a ghost
Sticking their tongues out of a window.
Every house in Palm Springs has a bit of
My seed flowered throughout their dry lawn.
Every house in Palm Springs plucks a piece
Of my swollen tongue until nothing's left.
Every house in Palm Springs breaks a shard
Of glass that shouldn't be there to begin with.
Every house in Palm Springs spreads me,
Just a bit, until I call onto all four corners and
Isn't this what invincibility is meant to feel like?
Every house in Palm Springs knows death.
Every house in Palm Springs knows the song
To my well sought-out eulogy.
Every house in Palm Springs has punched
My knees with a meat cleaver for a rise.
Every house in Palm Springs has a Palm Tree
That doesn't belong there like so many others.
Every house in Palm Springs, I've sold you
A bit of my body and I am here to cash out.
Every house in Palm Springs, you know,
You know I am exhausted, right?
Every house in Palm Springs I've met your
Beautiful pupils dipped in black paint.
Every house in Palm Springs, I don't want to go
Down that forked road once again.
Every house in Palm Springs has a hill of
bodies growing somewhere in their backyard.
Every house in Palm Springs, shut up, I'm talking.

He Wants to Have a Conversation On Rolling Veins

Because the moon was out that night,
And very still, and spoke of promises
With its very stillness so I had to listen.
As I was listening, I imagined the ocean
During high-tide, and how somewhere
In California the waves were destructive
Enough to wipe out an entire home, but
I was more focused on the ebb and flow
Of the very thing inside of his veins
Ready to obliterate his soft, soft voice
That was so earnest in its story-telling.
This man could have taught me of love
But as I returned the next morning
He was nothing more than soot and ash.
And as I listened to the waves rolling
In and out, in and out, in and out
Because the moon was out that night,
I remembered him asking for a way out.

Imagine Being That Elegant

He places a torch and his tongue in my hand.
He places a cock and a gun down my throat.
He places some meth and his spit on the tip
of my tongue and asks me to speak until I've

Turned this situation into some form of song.
He places a serrated knife in my back pocket
And whispers that I'm weak and nimble and
Someday I might be beautiful enough for him.

He places an oil burner on my thighs that had
Been burning for the last two-hundred days
And says *Wherever this scar goes you'll take*
Me with you and here he is: tongue ripped out.

He places many stories in my mouth, none of
Which would have belonged to me until he put
a small, red torch and his tongue in my palm.
I hope every time I open my mouth, you'll hear
How I've turned his situation into a form of song.

I Was

I was
in a big house,
full moon,
directionless.
but I was safe.
And the birds.

There was a fluttering in the chest
but it was teeth falling down a flight
of stairs mistaken for a case of wings.

I was
in a big house,
many rooms,
no stars, &
assumed safety.
And the hands.

The mangoes were ripe and a thief
stole all but one sweet, plump infant
right from the branches of his tree.

I was
in a big house,
no rooms,
many lights, &
my breathing.
And the murder.

To de-feather a bird one must first
kill. So they killed the bird. A million
birds fell from the empty night sky.

I was
in a big house,

full moon,
like a ripe melon.
Many rooms,
let me keep you
safe. Go, run.

ABOUT THE AUTHOR

Anthony Aguero is a queer writer in Los Angeles, CA. His work has appeared, or will appear, in the *Carve Magazine, Rhino Poetry, 14 Poems, Redivider Journal, Foglifter,* and others.

Acknowledgements

Deepest gratitude to the editors of the following publications where these poems first appeared.

Heavy Feather Review - "Christian"
Okay Donkey Mag - "Hierarchy of Hunger"
Carve Magazine - "Papier-Mache"
FU Review - "My Body"
Rust and Moth - "Undetectable Explained to a Primo"
December Magazine - "Litany of Making Love When It'll Kill You"
Lumiere Review - "Tía"
14 Poems - "His Profile Says He Is Hunting"
Redivider Poetry - "My Therapist Asks Why I Didn't Deserve the Assault"
North of Oxford - "Ezequiel"
Cathexis Northwest Press - "Sometimes I Feel Like a Fraud" and
"Someone Says They'd Take a Bullet for You"
Rhino Poetry - "Everyone Wants to Tell Me How to Be Alone"
Yemassee Journal - "The Shape of My Dreams"
Maudlin House - "You Can Do Anything for 30 Days"
Storm Cellar - "Today I Offer Something Tender"
Emerge Literary Journal - "Human Immunodeficiency Virus"
Leon Literary Review - "I Would've Done Anything" &
"The Leaves in the Tree Are Looking a lot Like Shadows"
Night Heron Barks - "O These Titles We Inherit"
Contemporary Verse 2 – "Self-Appraisal"
Foglifter Journal – "I Was"
Dreginald – "A Man Relapsed with Me"

I am immensely grateful to Manuel Gonzalez, Randy James, Ben Kline, Giovanni Adams, Douglas Lantis, Dustin Newcombe, Omar Nieto and Travis

Tate for being either a person who has allowed me to grow with them when I came in from the cold grip of drug abuse and led me to the completion of this collection or has been another eye of guidance in the process of working on this collection.

Many thanks to the poets whose work I've read that has allowed me to challenge and shape my voice into the poet I want to be – there are far too many.

Notes

The quote by Louise Glück is *Scattered Thoughts* from her collection *Mutable Earth*.

The quote by Jean Valentine is *For love*, from her collection *Door in the Mountain*.

The quote by Natalie Diaz is *exhibits from The American Water Museum* from her collection *Postcolonial Love Poem*.

The lyrics in *My Therapist Asks Why I Think I Didn't Deserve the Assault* are from "Dream a Little Dream of Me" originally written by Gus Kahn with music by Fabian Andre and Wilbur Schwandt.

CPSIA information can be obtained
at www.ICGtesting.com
Printed in the USA
LVHW080538010522
717430LV00004B/134